Financially Smart Business

An action-oriented framework for turning information overwhelm and confusion into clarity, confidence, and financial results for your profitable business

Felicia Lee

BASc, MBA, CFP®, CLU®, CKA, FEA®, CEPA®

Principal, Clarity Planning Inc.

Published by Prominence Publishing.
www.prominencepublishing.com

Financially Smart Business/Felicia Lee. -- 1st ed.
ISBN: 978-1-990830-14-3

Contents

Free Resources

Having ideas, frameworks, and ways of thinking without relevant tools that are actionable is short-sighted.

That's why I've prepared the following resources for you as you read this book:

The Financially Smart Business Framework

I find that seeing the big picture on a single page is helpful to understand how all the different components fit in. If you would enjoy having the Financially Smart Business Owners Framework for reference, you can download the infographic here: www.financiallysmartbusiness.com.

FINANCIALLY SMART BUSINESS FRAMEWORK

⊂⊃ Clarity

A-TEAM

Assemble your team of advisors who work collaboratively so that your personal and business tax, legal, and financial planning affairs are well integrated and taken care of.

CASH FLOW

Shift how you allocate your cashflow and order of spending so that you have surplus to fund future goals.

PROVISION

Life is unpredictable, but how you provide for your loved ones doesn't have to be. Learn how much they need, what you can afford, and where best to provide funds from.

MARGIN

Plan for the future through creating financial margins, making smart money decisions, and building short and long-term goals

OWNERSHIP

Establish financial goals, create appropriate business structures and accountability measures to track and guide your decision making.

VISION

Discern what type of business you want to build and align your financial strategies to your growth plans.

Visit financiallysmartbusiness.com for more information and resources

The Financially Smart Business Assessment

You may be wondering where you are financially, and if you are on the right path towards your personal and business financial goals. Understanding your current progress will help you see where to go next.

The Financially Smart Business Assessment will show you where you are now, what you may be missing, and what to focus on next.

You can find the assessment on www.financiallysmartbusiness.com.

The assessment takes 5 minutes and the results will be emailed to you.

Collaborative Discovery Session

It can be tough to figure out how all the financial planning pieces fit together. Not every advisor understands the full picture of your vision, and it can be confusing to know how to put all of these pieces together. We understand the value of talking through your financial situation with someone qualified, especially when it involves understanding your business and personal finances, in a warm, compassionate, judgement-free zone.

If you would like to schedule this discovery session, simply answer a few questions at financiallysmartbusiness.com and we look forward to connecting with you.

You don't have to figure this out on your own. Most business owners I know prefer to focus on growing their business, and to have external support to ensure strategies are in place to monitor and manage their business and personal finances.

The Collaborative Discovery session is a conversation to get clear on what exactly you need to do in order to have clarity, confidence, and control of your finances.

We are here to serve you when the timing is right for you – whether it is right now, or after you have finished reading a few chapters, or once you've finished the whole book – schedule your Collaborative Discovery session here: www.financiallysmartbusines.com

Praise

"Felicia and her team are awesome! I can sleep peacefully at night knowing that our finances are in order and we have a solid retirement plan for our future."

~ Dat Wong, DW & Company, CPA

"Felicia has been helping me with my financial planning as it relates to my physiotherapy business as well as my own personal planning. I have felt extremely well supported with the guidance and expertise that Felicia has been able to provide. I have learned an incredible amount from her and I have felt very empowered to make educated decisions for myself and my business.

Felicia has been extremely thorough in evaluating all aspects of my financial journey and has really helped me to look at the big picture and helping me to put it all together. I would genuinely recommend Felicia's services and will continue to work with her as my business and personal finances evolve."

~ Silvana Echeverri, Kids Physio Group

"A close friend recommended Felicia when we were looking for a financial planner and we could not be more pleased with Felicia. We have been working together for the past two years. She has shown us how to prepare for our retirement as it approaches and also helped us with our purchase of our home on Vancouver Island. Her knowledge of the financial markets is getting us excellent returns on our investments. We would highly recommend Felicia to anyone who is looking for a financial planner."

~ George and Patti Martin, Well Balanced Design

"Before working with Felicia, I had no idea that a financial planner who focused on helping small business owners (like me) existed! Financial planning with Felicia means that what's happening in my business and my personal needs and wants are all considered, which makes all the difference to me feeling supported in my financial planning for the future. Meeting Felicia and her team were game-changers.

Felicia is one of those rare gems who is knowledgeable and caring. She makes every effort to ensure that I'm making the right financial planning choices for the vision I have for my business and personal life and into my golden years. Knowing that my financial planning is in such good hands gives me peace of mind."

~ Audrey Kwan, AJK Consulting Inc.

Preface

Is this the book for you?

You've worked hard for the last number of years, and finally, you are no longer in survival mode. You've figured out how to market, sell, and generate revenues consistently in your business, and deliver your services or products to a growing number of happy customers. When you log in to your company bank account, you are often proud of yourself for the number that you see, even if you know you have room to grow. You're making money, you are grateful that there is enough to pay yourself consistently each month, and the balance in your bank account feels healthy and seems to be growing.

But perhaps at the back of your mind, you're still not completely sure if you're financially okay. Here are some questions that may have come up:

- Should I pay myself more or just keep the money in the business?

- Am I putting enough money away for my retirement?

- How fast should I grow my busincss?

- What should I do with the cash sitting in my business bank account? It's just sitting there and seems like a waste.

- Should I reinvest more cash into expanding the company?

- Should I buy more RRSP or TFSA? Which one is better for me?

- Should I start a holding company?

- Will I have enough to pay for my kids' education?

- Should I buy an investment property?

- Can I be more generous in my giving?

- Do I have enough?

- Am I okay financially?

You've tried asking your advisors a few of these questions, and even though they've tried to answer as best as they can, you're not completely confident you've got things figured out financially. Sometimes you wonder if you are even asking the right questions – you feel like you don't know what you don't know, so it's difficult to know how to tie all the financial pieces in your business and in your personal life together. When it comes to the money stuff, it just seems complicated and confusing.

There was a time when your only focus was marketing and generating sales for your business, and now that your business has grown, with more opportunities and also more expenses to account for, you don't feel like you're being all that strategic with your money. You have some idea of how to budget and allocate your finances, but you're so caught up with the busyness of running the business and your life, you don't know how to figure out the strategies to have financial clarity.

If this is you, here's what you need now to gain clarity and confidence in your financial planning:

Financially Smart Business Framework

When you are strategic about your finances, you become a wise steward of the resources that are given to you to manage – this allows you to grow and scale your company, provide for those that you love and causes that you believe in, and gives you flexibility and freedom for your future.

Regardless of what type of business you have, your industry, or your personal and family situation, there are reasons why it's difficult for business owners to figure out how to be smart and strategic in their financial decision making. First of all, financial planning was never taught in school. Although you may have vague memories of making fictitious budgets in your high school consumer education class many years ago, that's hardly similar to the money decisions you are making today. Second of all, you likely have a number of current advisors helping you with the various topics surrounding money: an accountant to help you with your company and personal tax filing, someone in the bank that helps you with your investments, and perhaps an insurance agent that you bought some life insurance policies from some years ago, but you haven't seen them since then. None of these advisors communicate with each other, so you're left to figure out how to piece together all the advice you're given ... yet you were never taught how.

The reality is, what got you here won't get you to the next level.

In order to relieve the confusion and complexity of making decisions about your finances, you'll need a new framework to tie all these financial planning pieces together that lines up with your specific goals, your values, and your priorities. You need the Financially Smart Business Framework.

What is the Financially Smart Business Framework?

Picture an orchestra about to play a symphony. String instrument players surround a tall conductor who stands on a podium, and woodwind players and brass players sit on risers behind. Each musician needs to play well, but this alone is not enough. If one section of the orchestra is not listening or aware of what another section of the orchestra is doing, you don't hear the flow of beautiful rhythm and notes, but instead what feels like noise and clashing sounds. Similarly, each of the financial planning areas is like one type of instrument in the orchestra, each area needs to complement and flow together to make your finances work for you.

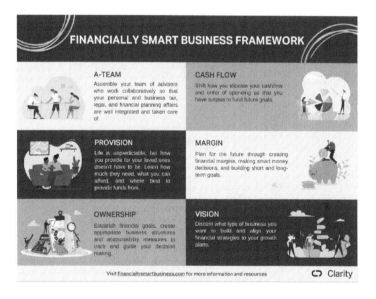

FINANCIALLY SMART BUSINESS FRAMEWORK

A-TEAM
Assemble your team of advisors who work collaboratively so that your personal and business tax, legal, and financial planning affairs are well integrated and taken care of.

CASH FLOW
Shift how you allocate your cashflow and order of spending so that you have surplus to fund future goals.

PROVISION
Life is unpredictable, but how you provide for your loved ones doesn't have to be. Learn how much they need, what you can afford, and where best to provide funds from.

MARGIN
Plan for the future through creating financial margins, making smart money decisions, and building short and long-term goals.

OWNERSHIP
Establish financial goals, create appropriate business structures and accountability measures to track and guide your decision making.

VISION
Discern what type of business you want to build and align your financial strategies to your growth plans.

Visit financiallysmartbusiness.com for more information and resources   ⊂⊃ Clarity

What you should know is that the current silo approach to finances is very common. Most of our clients were in this situation before they found us. The process you'll find in the following pages is your road map to integrating all these pieces together.

Enjoy, and know that we're here for you when you need us.

If You're Not Yet Profitable in Your Business

If you haven't yet reached enough sales in your business to be profitable or to pay yourself consistently, some of these strategies may not feel applicable. If that's the case, your focus is to increase sales and get more clients. It may still be important to focus on having strategies to protect what you're building, which are outlined in Chapter 3. Once you're profitable and can pay yourself, you will gain much more from the discussion within these pages.

The author is Canadian. Does this book still apply if you don't live in Canada?

First of all, I'm so sorry … that you don't live in this beautiful country.

Yes, you are welcome to read the book, but please note that while some of the general financial principles and strategies are good practices for anyone and can be applied to business owners in different countries, when it comes to financial, tax, and legal planning, counsel should be sought from advisors licensed in your jurisdiction to achieve best results. The principles in this book are specifically suited to business owners and families residing in Canada.

Introduction

I was driving my car downtown on a summer day in 2014. I was a business coach then, having just celebrated having 200 small business owners work with me to grow and scale their companies. I was feeling particularly grateful that I was able to do this for a living, helping clients grow their revenues and scale their businesses. I had just found a parking spot in downtown Vancouver, and was figuring out how best to weave my way through some construction road closures and pedestrian detours to not be late to a networking event (I hate being late!)

Then a sight caught me by surprise and abruptly stopped my hurried steps. About a block away from my destination was a makeshift pedestrian walkway, where the typical thin plywood barriers had a window cut-out - the developer of the upcoming new hotel and residential tower had made a window where passersby could peek into what was happening on the other side of the wire fencing.

I peeked into the window and gasped at the massive hole that burrowed into the ground. It must have been about four to five stories deep and one whole city block wide. I stopped for several minutes, watching the incredible feat of construction workers in excavators digging up the ground efficiently, where a small lineup of trucks along the constructed dirt ramp waited to carry tonnes of earth away. "The taller a building is, the deeper they need to dig to make a strong foundation," I thought to myself.

Almost immediately, another thought came to me. "You are working with your clients focusing solely on building and growing, just like constructing taller and taller skyscrapers. But what are their foundations like?" I was painfully reminded of a recent coaching session with a client, Julie (name changed for privacy).

Julie owned a documentary film company that worked with mid to large corporations and foundations in Canada and the US to capture the sustainability and charitable impact these organizations were making in their communities. It was a dream for her to be working with international clientele, building her team of videographers and production assistants, and making stunning videos to raise funds, truly making a difference for her clients and their stakeholders. She had just hit 7-figure revenues from landing contracts with a few large foundations in the US, and had recently signed a lease for an 8,000 square foot office in downtown Vancouver, with a sweeping view of the Burrard Inlet. Her team was creating amazing work and referrals, and requests were coming in from across the US to work with her.

These were all goals that she set and we had worked on diligently over the last few years. We had successfully implemented marketing and referral strategies, built processes and systems for company operations, built a team that enabled her to delegate operations and administrative items so she could focus on strategic growth, and by all counts, it was going really well. Or so I thought.

We had typically done our coaching session via phone or Skype as she travelled so much, but that summer she was in town, so we arranged to meet for our coaching session in person at her new downtown office. It was late in the afternoon and her team had left for the day, and she first gave me a tour of the office before we sat down in her conference room, facing the beautiful harbour with cruise ships and tourists filling the streets below.

We had planned for that session to go over big picture goal setting for the next 3-5 years, since she had accomplished all the goals she set in the last two years. Anything was possible for her future, and I was truly excited. I got my notepad and pen ready, and looked at her and said "So, where do you want to go from here?"

Her eyes started filling with tears, and she said to me "I don't know, I don't think my business is going to make it." And she started sobbing.

We didn't end up discussing goals nor creating a future vision that afternoon. Instead, she shared with me how she just got notice from her accountant that she owes a large sum in taxes that she doesn't have money in the bank to cover. In fact, she wasn't sure if she had enough money to pay her staff that month since she had just paid off the bill for renovations for the new office and it came in higher than what she expected. "How can I not have money when I'm making so much money?"

Over that session, she asked a lot more questions:

- How much money do I need to make to be able to cover everything?

- I've been working hard for so long and finally was able to give myself a raise last year. Do you think I should keep paying myself this amount when it seems that the company always needs more money to grow?

- Who can help me figure out how to make sense of the business financials? I'm really good with the creative side of the business and growing the company but the money side doesn't really make sense to me.

- Will I be ok financially? Do you think I can recover from this?

I didn't have answers to any of these questions at the time. I was shocked that a company that was doing well, making 7 figures, could struggle financially. I was confused about why she was caught by surprise – are these not things that her accounting, financial, or banking advisors would cover with her? I was also embarrassed that we had solely focused on the marketing, growth, and operations of the business, with me assuming that she knew all the financials. In the two years I worked with her, I never once asked her about the finances of her company or her personal financial goals as it was "outside" of our scope of services. Clearly, if the finances aren't taken care of, the business cannot grow.

After that coaching session with Julie, I thought a lot about the finances of business owners. I asked many of my clients afterwards – "How are you financially?" and to my surprise, many of them didn't confidently know how they were doing. They knew the sales they were generating, how much was in their bank accounts, had accountants and bookkeepers who helped them do their taxes, and even had some savings and investments built up for retirement. But they still weren't sure they were doing ok financially.

To be honest, at the time, I didn't know if I was doing well financially either. From the outside, it would appear that I had all the elements to figure it out. With an engineering degree and an MBA, numbers certainly were not strangers to me. My parents had even taught me from a young age to save money.

In my twenties, I dated an engineer that loved the stock markets, and our hobbies included taking securities courses in our spare time (we were real nerds). The biggest benefit of taking those courses was realizing that keeping track of what's happening in the markets would take a lot of time and expertise, and I wasn't going to master it from taking a few courses. I figured it would probably make the most sense to have a professional take care of it.

So, I looked up names of investment professionals in Vancouver, made several appointments to "interview them" and then learned that there was a thing called "minimum investable assets" and that I was nowhere close to meeting it and being able to work with anyone.

Finally, after being persistent and making even more appointments at various investment counsel firms, I found someone that worked in an independent firm that took pity on me. He took me on as a client despite not having much to start with, and managed my "funds" for me for the next decade.

But even with a head start, I still wasn't sure whether or not I was doing ok. Was I on the right pace, having enough savings to retire? How much should my business generate and how much should I put away versus investing it back into the company in marketing efforts to grow? Was I paying too much tax? Should I pay myself a salary or dividends? There were so many questions and yet I felt that I probably didn't even know what the right questions were to ask, never mind whom to ask these questions.

So back to that sunny day in downtown Vancouver where I was running late to the networking event. It occurred to me looking through the window down into the construction site – financials in a company are like the foundation of a tall building – it isn't sexy, it isn't visible to the outside world, and most business owners aren't really that excited about it. But to build a tall skyscraper, it better be in good shape, otherwise the business owner would be working with shaky foundations and won't feel confident in their business' strength.

I did not know at that time that soon after, I would transition my career to become a financial planner to business owners and their families.

In the spring of 2015, at a meeting with my mentor, she asked me how my business was going. The business was great, I said, but I had been running solo for 6 years and shared that I felt a bit lonely – as a sole business owner of a coaching practice, there were days where I wished I had a business partner to bounce things off or share the workload. It seemed like there was a crossroad ahead of me

– do I continue to grow my business on my own with a small team of assistants, or should I look into working with partners and have more support in the strategic thinking and planning side of the business. She said to me "Well, I'm looking for a successor, are you interested?"

My mentor had been in the insurance and financial planning business for over 25 years. I had always loved her office, her staff and the family-like atmosphere whenever I visited her at work. She had grown her business from the ground up and her clientele included business owners, professionals, and their families. They had served the 3rd generation of families with very little turnover because of their amazing customer service. Award plaques and trophies glazed their conference rooms.

Although I've always admired my mentor for her accomplishments and expertise, what I loved even more was her character and generosity – she was a major donor of not just money, but her time and her talents to causes that she loved and cared about. Beyond being a leader and a successful business woman, she had a beautiful family and was very much involved in the community. She was a wife, a mother to two amazing young adults, and a philanthropist.

"You mean if I join your business, I can learn from you everyday?" I thought and prayed about the opportunity, but really it seemed like a no brainer. I said yes a few weeks after, and over the next few months, transitioned my clients to other business coaches, and got my insurance licence.

The first few years in the new industry were tough but fulfilling. I worked with clients in the firm during the day, and at night, took financial planning courses, obtained certifications and learned as much as I could. Until I came into the industry, I had no idea what the alphabet behind a financial planner's name meant on their business cards. Now I know these meant hundreds to thousands of hours of learning the craft, for the benefit of providing competent advice for clients.

If you were looking at my business card, here is the list of alphabet soup and what all the terms mean:

BASc – Bachelor of Applied Science

My official undergraduate degree was in Electrical Engineering (Computer Option), which meant I did a lot of programming and advanced math courses. I often joke with clients that financial planning only requires working with "real" numbers, whereas in my engineering courses we had to deal with "imaginary" numbers in calculus classes. Which is perhaps why I'm no longer in engineering – I'm much better with dealing with real numbers in real life.

MBA: Master of Business Administration

In my MBA classes, we covered various areas of business administration topics such as accounting, applied statistics (yes there was still more math), human resources, business communication, business ethics, business law, strategic management, business strategy, finance, managerial economics, management, entrepreneurship, marketing, supply-chain management, and operations management. I love that in my financial planning conversations with clients, we not only talk about finances, but we go over business plans and challenges, to ensure that what we do in financial planning supports and aligns with our business strategies.

CFP®: Certified Financial Planner

According to FP Canada, the Certified Financial Planner® certification is the world's most recognized financial planning designation and is considered the 'gold standard' for the profession. CFP professionals have demonstrated the knowledge, skills, experience, and ethics to examine their clients' entire financial picture, at the highest level of complexity required of the profession. Generally, a CFP® professional can help a client with:

- Financial Management
- Insurance and Risk Management
- Investment Planning
- Retirement Planning
- Tax Planning
- Estate Planning
- Understanding Legal Aspects in a client's planning

CLU®: Chartered Life Underwriter

The CLU designation is conferred in Canada exclusively by The Institute for Advanced Financial Education ("The Institute™"). The Institute is the leading designation body in Canada for financial services practitioners in the specialty areas of Advanced Estate and Wealth Transfer, and Living Benefits.

The Chartered Life Underwriter (CLU) designation has been widely recognized for 90 years as a superior mark of excellence in the financial services industry. CLU designation holders are regarded as elite professional financial advisors who raise the bar in developing effective solutions for individuals, business owners, and professionals in the areas of risk management, wealth creation and preservation, estate planning, and wealth transfer.

FEA: Family Enterprise Advisor

The FEA designation is the benchmark in family enterprise advising. It's for professionals with significant technical knowledge to add to their skill set to better serve their family enterprise clients. FEAs use a multi-disciplinary approach where advisors integrate their own discipline with those of other professionals to provide collaborative and complementary advice to business family clients.

CKA®: Certified Kingdom Advisor

The CKA® Designation offers training and distinction to financial professionals who want to go deeper with their clients and their career. With this certification, financial advisors can elevate their practice to a higher level of expertise and understanding, as well as offer their clients peace of mind and purpose in stewarding their wealth.

CEPA®: Certified Exit Planning Advisor

The CEPA® Designation is conferred to advisors that help business owners align their business, personal and financial goals while building transferrable value into their company, so that the owner is always prepared to capitalize on a transition of their company, planned or unplanned.

To be clear, although these programs and certifications were very helpful in learning the craft of financial planning, what I found was that for business owners, financial planning is very different from others who don't own businesses. For instance, business owners have many choices to make with their money – you can choose to put all the profit you make back into the business or carve out a portion to pay yourself; you can pay yourself via salary or dividends or both, or not pay yourself at all if your spouse is making sufficient income to provide for family expenses; you can build wealth through growing your business or take a portion of the funds and invest in other assets like real estate, or invest in a different business.

To complicate the financial planning process further, you are typically working with multiple advisors in different areas of planning. For example, you may be working with an investment advisor, an accountant, a business coach or consultant, an insurance professional, and a lawyer. Typically, most of these professional advisors are working individually with the business owner and not in communication with each other in the various areas of planning. You are often left to tie all the pieces together.

As clients' businesses grew, what I realized was even more important in financial planning is to be able to integrate all of the areas of planning and coordinate between all these advisors, to ensure that advice in one area doesn't conflict with actions in another. My clients would often ask me to speak with their accountants, lawyers, and other advisors directly, coordinating on their behalf, because they didn't fully understand what the technical terms meant in these different meetings.

Over time, these conversations organically helped me to develop a framework and process of planning that enabled clients to see the bigger picture of how all their business and personal finances tied together. These frameworks covered each of the financial planning areas in detail, anticipated what decisions needed to be made, and helped clarify impacts and pros and cons of financial decisions for their future.

In the chapters that follow, I'll share these frameworks and processes with you, so that you may benefit from knowing how these financial planning areas fit together, know what questions to ask of your individual advisors, and determine how best to direct your financial resources to create the future that you hope for.

Shall we get started?

Chapter 1:
Assemble Your "A" Team

Action: Assemble your team of advisors who work collaboratively, so that your personal and business tax, legal, and financial planning affairs are well integrated and handled.

What Got You Here Won't Get You There is a book written by Marshall Goldsmith, a business coach and educator. While the content of the book is more targeted for corporate executives, the essence is that often, when we reach a certain level in our career, doing more of the same isn't going to get us ahead. We need to shift what we're doing to get to the next level.

For business owners, this also applies to financial planning. Typically, when business owners first approach me for financial planning, they are not starting from nothing. They already have a number of advisors helping them with the money side of their business and personal planning. They may have a bookkeeper or accountant or both helping them with their tax filing and keeping up to date on the financial side of their business. They may have some investments in the bank. They may have purchased some insurance policies, although it's often that they don't remember what they bought or know whether they should still continue to pay for these policies. Some may have even worked with a lawyer to incorporate their business, but perhaps haven't engaged a lawyer yet to look into their wills, even though they've been meaning to. Some may also have marketing consultants or business coaches that are helping them grow the revenue side of their businesses and building up their teams and operation systems.

The common theme is usually that none of the business owners' advisors typically know or work with each other. The tax, financial, investment, insurance, and legal planning are done independently and in silos, with the business owner being responsible for knowing what he/she needs to work towards, and trying to tie everything together. See below picture for how the business owner typically works with his/her advisors.

There are a few challenges with doing financial planning in this manner.

First of all, the business owner may be receiving conflicting advice from different advisors and hence not sure what to do next. For example, here is a common scenario: the business owner's investment advisor suggests for the client to top up their RRSP contribution each year, however his/her accountant suggested that they contribute to their TFSA instead because they are in a low tax bracket.

Another common scenario is that a client's insurance advisor asks them to buy permanent life insurance policies that they can use in the future to draw from to fund the children's education and receive some tax deferral benefits, however their financial planner thinks that they should instead put the money in RESP to take advantage of government grants today.

The business owner is left to figure out what to do next, and typically they don't have the time to figure out all the technical details and so even if they make a decision and listen to a suggestion from one advisor, they later wonder if they've made the right decision.

Sometimes a business owner isn't sure whether the advice is made with their best interest at heart - for example, when an investment advisor recommends that their client use surplus funds to invest into the stock market in lieu of paying down their mortgage, can the client be sure that there isn't a conflict of interest?

Another challenge for the business owner is that the financial industry is filled with specialists that only provide advice within their lane of expertise (as they should). This requires the business owner to engage multiple advisors for the different areas of planning. It is usually very confusing for the business owner to know what questions to ask or whom to ask when they have a question that spans multiple areas of planning. For example, a simple and common question that comes up is, "How much dividend or salary should I pay myself?" The answer to this question is anything but simple and depends on a number of factors:

- How much does the business owner need on a regular basis to cover personal cash flow needs?

- What are the corporation vs personal tax rates for the business owner and potentially his/her spouse's tax situation? What should be done to optimize their tax planning?

- What is the business owner's retirement plan – do they need to opt in to Canada Pension Plan (CPP)?

- Does the business owner need some salary income to qualify them for an upcoming mortgage or insurance approval?

- Where is best for the business owner to accumulate savings? Should they do it within the corporation or pay themselves more to accumulate wealth personally?

These are just a number of factors to consider – there may be even more factors to consider depending on if the client has other sources of income, real estate rental property and expected future rental income in retirement, or expected future inheritance or gifts. It is also necessary to consider a client's family make up - do they have spouses that own a business, or are employed through a different company? For many clients in the "sandwich" generation, they are not only taking care of their own families with children, but also need to take care of their parents. Many know they are named executors on their parents' wills, but are not really sure what that means, while others don't yet have the opportunity to discuss estate planning with their parents, yet they know that by default, they will end up handling all their parents' affairs once their parents pass away.

As businesses grow and needs become more complex, a business owner may not realize that they need more complex planning and can benefit from a higher level of expertise. Consider the following scenario: a child may start off playing soccer, coached by their teacher at school or by a parent coach in their after-school soccer league. As they develop to a higher level of playing, they may then be working with an amateur youth coach. At the college level, a soccer player may have specific coaches for skills like corner kicks, first touch, free kicks, heading, and different coaches for fitness and conditioning. At the professional level, a team may have a head coach, assistant coaches, specific skills development coaches, a goalkeeper coach, fitness trainers, physiotherapists, and sports medicine doctors.

In business, as the company grows, the business owner may also benefit from having a team of advisors with more specialized skill sets. Typically, profitable businesses may benefit from a team of advisors working together to cover each of the following business and personal areas of financial planning (see table below):

Advisor	Specialty
Accountant	Personal and corporate tax advice and planning
	Accounting – preparing financial statements, forecasts and budgeting
	Bookkeeping – payroll, accounts receivables and payables, bank reconciliation, inventory management
	Advisory services on business structures, tax implications of financial decisions
	Chief Financial Officer (CFO) Services
Lawyer	Incorporation
	Shareholder agreements
	Advice on business structures
	Contracts for employees, contractors, or clients
	Legal counsel for disputes
	Freezes and roll-over transactions
Wills and Estate Lawyer	Wills
	Powers of Attorney
	Trusts formation and planning
Financial Planner	Financial management
	Cash flow management
	Insurance and risk management
	Investment planning
	Retirement planning
	Tax and estate planning
Investment Advisor	Investment advice and management
	Portfolio asset allocation

Advisor	Specialty
Insurance Advisor	Life, disability, critical illness insurance
	Business interruption insurance
	Errors and Omission insurance
	Property losses insurance
	General liability insurance
	Home and vehicles insurance

When assembling your team of advisors, you may wish to determine whether they are appropriate for your stage of business and planning needs. Here are some questions that you may want to consider asking your advisors and determine if the answers meet your needs and preferences:

- Are they familiar with your industry and current business stage planning needs?

- What do they foresee as planning needs for you personally and in your business now and in the next 3, 5, 10, 20 years?

- Are they working with businesses that are larger or further along than yours, and can they provide advice proactively to help you prepare for the next stage of your business?

- Do they typically work with clients' other advisors in a collaborative manner? If so, who typically do they expect to lead the multi-disciplinary process or discussion?

- How often do they suggest meeting with you and with your other advisors? What topics do they suggest to cover those meetings?

Here is an example of a meeting rhythm you could consider developing with your advisors:

Advisor	Frequency of meeting	Topic to cover
Bookkeeper	Monthly	Bookkeeping Monthly financial snapshot of health of business
Accountant	Annually	Preparing Financial Statements Tax Filing Budget and forecasting
	As needed	Financial decision advice (e.g. hiring, major purchases, change of business structure)
Business Lawyer	Yearly	Year End Filing
	Every 3-5 years	Review shareholder agreement
	As needed	Updating corporate structure New contracts/employment/ client agreements New contracts for employees, contractors, clients New corporation set up Dispute resolution counsel

Advisor	Frequency of meeting	Topic to cover
		Corporate structure changes (new owners, freezes and rollovers)
Wills and Estate Lawyer	Every 3-5 years	Updating will and power of attorney (especially if there are changes in personal life and major life events)
Financial Planner	Annually	Adjustments and review if on track with financial/retirement plan
	As needed	Changes in personal life or business that impact financial planning New business or personal goals
Investment Advisor	Quarterly or Semi-Annually	Market Update Portfolio performance review
	Annually	Discuss RRSP/TFSA/Non-Registered amounts to contribute personally Corporate investment planning
	As needed	Personal or company changes that change existing risk profile and timeframe of investments
Insurance Advisor	Every 3-5 years	Review amount of coverage and type of plan if still appropriate for current personal/business situation

Advisor	Frequency of meeting	Topic to cover
	As needed	Changes in business (increase in risk/liability, new employees/partners, expansion into new locations)
		Personal life event (e.g. new child, marriage/divorce, death in family, new home purchase)

In addition to meeting with your advisors individually, here are also some examples of situations where joint meetings with multiple advisors are beneficial, so that cross-disciplinary issues and items can be discussed collaboratively:

Advisors	Frequency	Topics
Accountant, Financial Planner, Investment Advisor	Annually	Determine amount of salary/dividend to pay yourself
		Determine most efficient investment vehicle – how much to contribute into RRSP vs. TFSA vs. Personal or Corporate Non-registered plans
Accountant, Lawyer, Financial Planner	As needed	Holding company and trusts planning
		Major asset purchases or sales

Advisors	Frequency	Topics
Accountant, Financial Planner, Insurance Advisor	As needed	Ownership structure of insurance policies (personal or corporate owned)
Financial Planner, Investment Advisor	As needed	Retirement planning
Accountant, Financial Planner, Insurance Advisor, Lawyer	As needed	Succession planning, estate planning

It is helpful to have one of your advisors act as your "lead" advisor to coordinate the planning and meetings with your other advisors. For example, in the medical field, this is the family physician. Your family physician knows your overall health condition and medical history, and refers and works with specialists as needed to diagnose and provide specialized medical counsel and recommendations. The family physician understands complex medical terminology and can effectively communicate directly with specialists, and provide follow up care and continue monitoring of patients over time.

Based on the current stage of your business, here are some questions to consider:

- Who are your current advisors for your personal and business financial planning?

- On a scale of 1 to 10, with 1 being "none at all" and 10 being "completely", how much are your current advisors collaborating with each other? How much would you like them to collaborate with each other?

- Are there any advisors missing from your current team that you would benefit from their counsel?

- Who can act as the financial "family physician" for you and your business?

- What members do you need to add to your advisor "A team" to give you a full picture of your financial planning?

For a PDF copy of the "A Team" and a list of questions to ask each advisor, visit www.financiallysmartbusiness.com.

Chapter 2:
How Much is Enough?

> **Action: Shift how you allocate your cash flow and order of spending so that you have surplus to fund future goals.**

How much is enough? When it comes to money and how much disposable income we want to have each month – is there an amount that is enough? Or is more always better?

When I was a business coach, one of the first questions clients filled in in their intake form was their business goals. Typically most clients would write down their revenue target – "I want to have $200,000 in sales this year" "I want to build a 7-figure company and aim for $1,000,000 in sales" The ones that didn't put down revenue goals typically still wrote something about achieving a certain financial objective "I want to make enough revenues to pay myself $8,000 per month" etc.

When clients achieve these goals, we would celebrate ... and then set new revenue goals and discuss the strategies and plans to meet those over the next year. I can't recall one single client that said, "I think I'm good now and don't need to make any more", regardless of hitting $1M or $5M or $10M in sales each year.

While this worked pretty well for me then as a business coach because clients would continue to retain me to meet their next year's business objectives, what became increasingly clear to me was that there was no number that was "enough."

Each client usually had a number that they thought they wanted to achieve, however it was as if we were chasing the horizon... as we reached the target, the goalpost would then move because clients did not feel that they had "arrived," and they typically still needed to make more money.

The fact was that as revenues increased, expenses often also increased. There is always something that needs funding: hiring another staff member, increasing inventory, leasing a bigger office to house everything, or upgrading systems and infrastructure to support the growth. Even though clients could pay themselves more and often did so, the act of reaching a certain level of revenues often came with increased expenditures as well.

In my financial planning work with clients, they would sometimes spend the extra personal income on new purchases – a new car, a longer vacation, renovations or moving to a new home. Sometimes it isn't even about being extravagant – just a nicer restaurant to enjoy on weekends, eating out slightly more frequently, and buying nicer stuff here and there because they can afford it now.

What is really interesting though is that clients often don't feel significantly happier just because they have a bigger business or they can pay themselves more. So many clients have mentioned to me that they thought they would be happier if they achieved a certain financial goal or reached a business milestone, but in reality, most don't feel too different when their businesses become more established.

Does having more money equal more happiness? One would think so. Hence the richest countries of the world should produce the happiest citizens, right? And yet we know that this isn't necessarily the case. Dr. Jorge Yamamoto has made his life's work about understanding happiness, and his research shows that countries with the most wealth tend to actually be the least happy!

(https://www.guelphhumber.ca/news/exploring-happiness-around-world)

In our culture, we are taught and wired to be discontent. In fact, the whole field of marketing could be considered as the exercise of making you aware of what you aren't currently doing or what you don't yet have, and that if you bought the gadget or the product, you would be happier and be better off. Hence, we can always convince ourselves that we "need" another pair of shoes, a newer model of something we already have, or another "experience" because we deserve it.

While there is nothing inherently wrong about trying to make our lives a bit better, the key is knowing that achieving more or having more only satiates us temporarily. The answer to "How much is enough?" is not that there is a magic amount of wealth that will make us happy – if so, all celebrities and the wealthy and rich would be the happiest people in the world – which we know is not the case. Our culture would have us believe that the more we have, the more content we feel; however, this is really a lie.

Contentment is actually a choice – something that we choose.

This is somewhat counter-cultural, however, mastering this allows one to not fall into the trap of feeling like they are never making enough and never having enough.

Does that mean you shouldn't choose to grow your business once it hits a certain level? Or you shouldn't aim to make more money once you can cover your expenses?

Choosing contentment doesn't mean that you "play small" or don't aim to grow.

For example, a few years ago, one of my clients, Jonathan, sold his business for enough money that paid off his mortgage and allowed him enough funds to never worry about his retirement. He was elated for a few weeks, and then in our meeting, seemed a bit lost – he mentioned he didn't really know what to do with himself or where to go next. He had been an entrepreneur all his life and couldn't imagine "retiring" early, and wasn't sure what to do next. He had some ideas about a few businesses he could launch, but didn't seem as excited.

I asked him, "If you could build another company, what could you use the money for? What are you passionate about?" He paused for a bit, and then his eyes lit up. It turns out that he has a passion to support his church – in fact, he donated a significant portion of proceeds from his company's sale to help build a new church campus. I asked, "What if you were to continue to do what you love – building and growing companies – and use the funds to fund building new churches?"

That changed everything. The spark came back immediately and we went over his business ideas and created goals and strategies and plans for them. It's been several years since then, and he is currently in the process of negotiating the pricing and terms to sell his 2nd business to a strategic buyer, while putting plans in place to launch the 3rd business. In a recent conversation, he mentioned he couldn't be happier. He is doing what he loves best – being an entrepreneur in starting and growing businesses, but with a different Why. The purpose of the funds is now to give to causes and organizations that he loves and supports, instead of falling into the trap that making more and having more would bring lasting happiness.

How much do I need to be content?

You may have a question – so how do I practically figure out how much to allocate to our lifestyle so that I can figure out what is "enough"?

Many don't really know how much money they are spending each month, let alone to be intentional about allocating an amount to it. Usually, we know the amount of income we make because it shows up in our bank account. Then money goes towards paying bills, and we hope to have some leftover each month.

I learned some of the best principles for money allocation from my CKA training, developed by Ron Blue, the founder of Kingdom Advisors. You can check out the organization here: https://kingdomadvisors.com/. What I loved about these principles is that they work well regardless of how much money you have and where you are along your financial planning journey.

Here is an overview of how to think about money allocation. Regardless of your stage of business or level of income, there are only 5 ways to use your money (see diagram below):

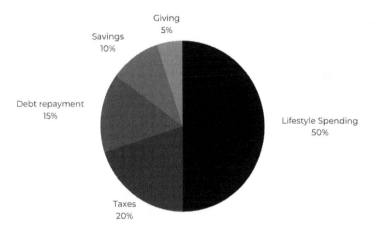

The 5 uses are:

1. Lifestyle spending

2. Paying taxes

3. Paying debt

4. Grow savings

5. Giving

The types of uses of money are illustrated in a pie chart because decisions you make (consciously or unconsciously) in one segment impact other segments. If you have more debt, you have less to spend in the other segments. If you dedicate a very large segment to lifestyle, you may not have enough to allocate to the other segments, and as a result, may need to go into more debt. Regardless of how much income you have, everyone has the same decisions to make – how much would I want to allocate to each segment for my spending?

Here are a few questions to consider:

1. What does your current pie-chart look like in terms of percentage allocation?

2. What do you want it to look like instead?

For many clients, it was eye-opening to do this exercise. Many did not realize how much they were paying in taxes nor how much they were spending each month to fund their lifestyle. Normally a large chunk went to paying mortgages and loans, income taxes, and lifestyle spending, with some leftover going to savings or giving. When asked, most would prefer to allocate more to savings or to be able to give at least a bit more, but they just don't feel that there is anything leftover to give at the end of each month.

Order of Spending

A possible cause of why this happens is related to the order in which we spend money. Without planning, this is usually the default order in which money goes out of our bank accounts:

1. Lifestyle – pay for groceries, food, household expenses, meals and entertainment

2. Pay debt – pay mortgage or rent, car loans, student loans

3. Pay taxes – pay income tax installments (this may have already been deducted from one's paycheck if income is from salary instead of dividends or owners' draw), property tax

4. Grow savings – increase savings in bank accounts, use investments for long term growth

5. Give – donations to charities

I don't know too many people that "accidentally" have a lot of leftover funds for the "Grow" and "Give" category. Usually there are more people that accidentally spend more on lifestyle, debt, or paying taxes.

A potential solution is simply to change the order in which we allocate our funds when it hits our bank accounts, for example in the following order:

1. Giving
2. Taxes
3. Debt
4. Grow
5. Lifestyle

What this means is that for each segment of the uses of money, we determine the amount we want to spend in that category, and we use the money first in that order, and then have the leftover allocated to the next category.

For example, if a business owner pays themselves $10,000 (gross salary) per month, they may ideally want to allocate as follows:

Percentage (Amount)	Category	Details
10% ($1,000)	Giving	Tithing and donations
20% ($2,000)	Taxes	Paying income taxes
25% ($2,500)	Debt	Mortgage payment
10% ($1,000)	Grow	Savings, investment contributions
35% ($3,500)	Lifestyle	Food, Utilities, Transportation, Clothing

However, if they were to take a closer look at what they are actually doing each month, the current reality may be as follows:

Percentage (Amount)	Category	Details
0% ($0)	Giving	Tithing and donations
30% ($3,000)	Taxes	Paying income taxes
25% ($2,500)	Debt	Mortgage payment
0% ($0)	Grow	Savings, investment contributions
45% ($4,500)	Lifestyle	Food, Utilities, Transportation, Clothing

In this scenario, there isn't money allocated to Giving and Growth because all the funds are used up in the Taxes, Debt, and Lifestyle category. The questions I may ask are:

1. Are you satisfied with how your funds are currently allocated?

2. What are the short term and long-term consequences of the current allocations?

3. If you are not satisfied with the allocation, what do you want it to be instead?

4. What would be the short term and long-term consequences of the desired allocations?

By no means am I saying that we should all dramatically change our spending and reign in our lifestyle expenses allocations (although sometimes this is absolutely the thing to do), but that we could be more intentional about aligning our spending and expenses with what is important to us and what we value, *if we knew* what we were spending our money on.

I would encourage you to check what your allocations are currently (you can go here – financiallysmartbusiness.com – to download a spreadsheet to track for the next few months) in order to become more aware of your current situation, and then determine if you want to change the allocations for the future.

Move (slowly) in the right direction

If it happens that your current budget allocation vs. your ideal budget allocation is far apart (e.g., more than 20% apart), I would encourage you to not make drastic changes within a short timeframe, unless you know yourself to be a person that can sustain drastic changes (good for you!)

A more practical, sustainable practice is to start small – maybe change 1% every 1-2 months in each category in the right direction, and over time, achieve the ideal allocation that you want to see. This would allow you to adapt to new habits over time.

Another suggestion is to speak with a financial planner that can further help you optimize your allocations. In meetings with our clients, we often notice that they are paying too much tax because of a lack of understanding of efficient tax planning, or that they have high-interest loans that can be consolidated into lower interest rate loans that can save hundreds to thousands of dollars each month.

Spending in Your Business

Within the business, tracking may be slightly easier because you may already have established bookkeeping and accounting systems to track monthly revenues and expenses in order to reach your profit goals. A similar exercise I would encourage you to do is to review your expenses periodically with your bookkeeper and accountant, to check whether spending in each category (for example: labour/salaries, materials, marketing, training, rent/leases, insurance, utilities, interest, professional fees, etc.) are in line with best practices for your stage of business in your specific industry.

When you review your business financials, a good practice is to track and report each category as a percentage of your revenues, so that over time, you can determine if the percentage of expenses is in line with your revenue growth over time. This can easily be done through most accounting software. As your company grows, you can then determine if the percentage of spending for each category is in line with the revenue growth, and adjust your budget accordingly to ensure that you remain profitable as revenues grow. We will cover more on how best to track your company's financial performance in Chapter 5.

Chapter 3:
Who Do I Need to Take Care of?

Action: Life is unpredictable, but how you provide for your loved ones doesn't have to be. Learn how much they need, what you can afford, and where best to provide funds from.

"If you were to be sick or pass away prematurely, what would you want to see happen with your family?"

As entrepreneurs, I believe most of us are an optimistic bunch that sees gaps as opportunities, and turns problems into solutions. The optimistic and "can-do-it-all" entrepreneur nature means that many of us don't expect anything bad to happen to our own health, our ability to make a living, or that our lives would be cut short at all.

And yet, the reality is that de-risking is one of the foundational aspects to building financial security and especially an important consideration for business owners, since so much of our assets are tied up in the business – which is something that cannot be converted into cash easily, even in good times. If sickness and death were to happen to the business owner and no provisions are in place for protection of the family's financial wellbeing, the impact can be drastic.

Insurance can be a very efficient vehicle to provide financial protection for a business owner and their loved ones. However, with all the different types of products in the market, it can be confusing to figure out what is appropriate for your situation.

How much insurance do I need?

One of the areas we assess for prospective clients is auditing their existing insurance plans, to see if anything needs to be adjusted. A question I often ask is – "Why did you buy this type of insurance plan and this amount?" The answer is usually "I don't remember, the insurance agent recommended it."

Sometimes, insurance plans were bought many years ago, and even though the client's situation has changed (they have since been married, had kids, started a business, etc.), the plans have not been reviewed or updated since the original insurance agent has either left the industry, or that they have not been in touch with the client since the policies were sold.

I have also seen cases where the client is inappropriately insured from a timing perspective. For example, they have placed expensive policies for their children (because the insurance agent told them it was cheap to buy for the kids while they are young) while they themselves are under-insured. While the policies would be valuable decades down the road once their children have children and perhaps need the financial protection, they haven't prioritized providing for their current spouse and children if something were to happen to them.

Types of Insurance

There are three major types of insurance to look into to protect your family:

1. Life Insurance

2. Critical Illness Insurance

3. Disability Insurance

Life insurance

There are different types of life insurance but most can be categorized into 2 major types:

1. Term
2. Permanent

Term life insurance is typically used to cover for needs for a set period of time, for example for 10 or 20 years, if one passes away prematurely. The coverage is to provide funds to pay off mortgage, provide income protection for family, and provide for expected expenses such as funeral or children' education costs. It is more affordable than permanent life insurance and hence more coverage can be purchased to cover higher amounts needed in earlier years while a business owner has a young family to provide for. This can be very helpful to pay off mortgages, and provide income for a surviving spouse and young family if the business is still in early stages and there isn't yet sufficient wealth accumulated to provide for the family in case of premature death.

Permanent life insurance is typically higher priced than term life insurance, because it provides lifelong coverage regardless of age. It is typically beneficial for estate planning and wealth transfer to future generations and has features such as guaranteed cash values or investment options built in.

Life insurance can also be owned within a corporation to provide protection for the business. Here are a few scenarios to consider corporate-owned life insurance:

- Buy-sell – for companies with multiple owners/partners, to fund the buy-out of shares if a partner passes away

- Key person – to protect your business from the death of a key person

- Debt protection – to provide coverage to pay off loans

Life Insurance Calculation

There are two major categories to consider including:

1. Liabilities and larger expected expenses, for example:

   - Principal home mortgage amount owing

   - (Optional) investment property mortgages

   - Outstanding personal loans/debt

   - Funeral expenses

   - Children's education expenses

2. Income replacement

   - An amount to provide a portion or full replacement of lost income to family for a number of years (for example until children are adults or have finished their post-secondary education)

There are several calculators available to do this calculation online that are summarized here: www.financiallysmartbusiness.com

Disability Insurance

Disability insurance provides a monthly payment to help replace income and cover expenses in case an illness or an injury prevents you from working for a period of time.

One of the most valuable assets a business owner has is actually their ability to earn income over the span of their career. Consider the table below that shows how much income is brought in by a business owner that pays themselves $70,000, $100,000, $150,000, or $200,000 of income per year to age 65, assuming 2.5% raise each year:

Income per Year	Age 35	Age 45	Age 55
$70,000	$3,073,189	$1,788,126	$784,237
$100,000	$4,390,270	$2,554,466	$1,120,338
$150,000	$6,585,405	$3,831,699	$1,680,507
$200,000	$8,780,541	$5,108,932	$2,240,676

Now imagine that if something happens (illness, injury, accident) and one cannot work for a few years, or worse, the incident or illness requires them to change their career. The above table also shows the potential amount of income that is lost over the period of time.

Disability insurance provides income replacement for the period of time where you cannot work. There is usually a monthly maximum that you can receive depending on your age and occupation. It is a very important part of insurance planning to provide for financial security in case of unexpected illnesses or injuries.

Critical Illness Insurance

Critical illness insurance is different from disability insurance in that the payment is in a lump sum instead of receiving monthly payments. In Canada, critical illness insurance gives you a lump-sum tax-free payment if you are diagnosed with a serious illness (for example: life-threatening cancer, heart attack, or stroke). Some plans will also provide access to medical experts to provide a second opinion on diagnosis, explain treatment options, or include counselling or family support services.

The amount to put into place depends on a few factors:

- Monthly expenses to cover: mortgage or rent, household expenses, food and groceries

- Additional healthcare costs: domestic help, treatment and recovery care, travel to seek alternate care or private medical treatments

- Lost income during treatment/recovery

- Spouse's lost income if they take a leave of absence

It is important to consider having critical illness insurance to provide an initial lump sum payment to cover immediate costs, as well as disability insurance to provide longer term ongoing monthly income replacement, in order to avoid having to dip into retirement savings. For many, it can be difficult to replace hard-earned after-tax savings after experiencing a serious illness, since they may not be able to return to work in the same capacity as they had before the illness.

What if I'm not insurable?

The thing about insurance is that it is only available to those that don't need it …yet. If you are healthy and don't have a family history of health conditions, it can be very cost effective to provide the protection needed for family and loved ones.

However, if this option isn't available for you because of your health or family history of medical conditions, you may need to seek out alternate insurance carriers and plans that provide coverage for those with existing health conditions, usually with higher premium costs. Some boutique carriers also offer guaranteed-issue policies that may work for your situation.

Unfortunately, if you are in a situation where you cannot obtain insurance, you will need to self-insure and adjust your financial planning to ensure you have liquidity (i.e., cash easily accessible) when you need it. This may mean setting aside more money in your savings account, or allocating an amount in your investments that is lower risk and can be liquidated in different market conditions. It also means that in your business, you may want to build in more reserves or contingencies if you can't work, or by avoiding committing to long-term expenses or leases that you are obligated to pay back for years if circumstances cause your revenues or income to fluctuate.

Chapter 4:
Reverse Engineer the Future

Action: Plan for the future through creating financial margins, making smart money decisions, and building short and long-term goals.

In Chapter 2 we explored the 5 different segments of money allocation and the order of spending. Regardless of how much income you are making, the principles of good money allocation remain the same. Some make a little more money so the "pie" is a little larger while others are just starting out so their "pie" is a little smaller.

Depending on the money decisions that you make, the pie either becomes smaller or gets larger over time. For example, if you don't manage your lifestyle, you may overspend in that category and need to go into debt. If this becomes a habit and the amount of debt keeps increasing, you end up paying more interest charges and having less to allocate to savings. On the other hand, you could increase the size of the pie by making wise money decisions. You could focus on increasing profit and consequently pay yourself a higher income, you could proactively do tax planning to reduce taxes payable, or you could work on managing your lifestyle spending. All these activities enable you to have more margin and surplus to allocate towards savings and investments. The "grow" part of the pie is the segment that will increase the size of the pie over time.

How much should I save each month?

Ideally, the amount you save each month is calculated through a retirement planning cash flow projection analysis. That means determining your desired lifestyle including income and expenses in retirement years, and working backwards to determine how much you should save each year, based on what you have currently in your savings and investments today. This calculation can usually be performed through financial planning software through your financial advisor.

One of the challenges with retirement planning for business owners is that, unlike someone that works as an employee, they don't typically retire from their job as a 65 year old, which is the typical number used for retirement projections. Because most entrepreneurs love what they do and have the ability to structure their business around their needs, they can choose to work for many more years, or still be involved in their business in a reduced capacity if they choose.

The downside of entrepreneurship is that they may also have invested most of their resources into the business over the years, paid themselves very little in order to focus on funding business growth, and in later years, if the business has not been structured to command good value for sale or exit, they end up needing to keep the business going in order to fund their lifestyle income (we will cover more on this in Chapter 6).

Regardless of whether you've completed a retirement planning analysis, when it comes to savings and investments, what I've found is that those who end up reaching their retirement goals are those that saved and invested consistently over a longer period of time and took advantage of the power of compound interest.

A little over a long time becomes a lot

Take a look at the table below that shows you how much you could save by putting in $500, $1,000, or $2,000 per month, with investment that grow on average by 6% per year over different periods of time:

Amount per Month	10 Years	20 Years	30 Years
$500	$81,940	$231,020	$502,258
$1,000	$163,879	$462,041	$1,004,515
$2,000	$327,759	$924,082	$2,009,030

Now compare that with the one-time deposit you would need to make in order to generate the same savings over the same periods:

One-time amount to match equivalent monthly savings amount			
Amount per month	10 Years	20 Years	30 Years
$500	$45,755	$72,033	$87,448
$1,000	$91,509	$144,067	$174,896
$2,000	$183,019	$288,133	$349,792

Isn't it incredible that if you invested $500 per month over 30 years, it is equivalent to you investing $87,448 today? Or that $2,000 per month for 30 years is equivalent to investing almost $350,000 today? That is the magic of "a little over a long time becomes a lot".

If you are reading and thinking "I don't have $2,000, or $1,000, or even $500 a month to put towards my savings", or that you don't have 20 or 30 years until retirement, don't be discouraged. Start with something small, and an amount you feel comfortable with. I often suggest clients to go with an amount that they thought was a little low but they probably wouldn't miss it because they could have easily spent that amount on something else.

Starting with something small will allow you to develop a good habit. In the first few years, the amount you save and the growth of the funds may not seem like a lot, however, after a few years, you'll really start to see the magic of compounding starting to show in your portfolio. In addition, as your business grows, you can decide whether you want to allocate more to your savings, so don't be discouraged by what seems like small beginnings now.

Within your business, it is also prudent to track your expenses against your income to measure profitability. A great resource on this topic is the book *Profit First* by Mike Michalowicz. In the book, Michalowicz shares practical strategies for business owners on prioritizing profit goals, such that what remains is apportioned for expenses, instead of the other way around, where profit is considered leftover of whatever expenses have been incurred.

Five Principles of Smart Money Decisions

Regardless of where you are in your personal or business finances, there are five principles of smart money decisions that allow you to grow your margin:

1. Spend less than you earn

2. Do proactive tax planning

3. Avoid debt

4. Save to meet short- and long-term goals

5. Be generous with your giving

These principles correspond to decisions that you make within each segment of the money allocation pie.

Principle 1: Spend less than you earn

This may seem obvious, but with our current culture where credit is available readily and where spending can happen easily with a few clicks and taps on our credit cards or phones, it is so easy to overspend.

Do you have a system of keeping track of your business and personal expenses? Are you working within a budget and are you keeping to it? If you are finding that you don't have sufficient surplus each month to allocate towards your savings, start by building a budget and keeping track of your expenses over a few months to see where you are currently.

Here is a list of resources for your budgeting that may be helpful: www.financiallysmartbusiness.com

Principle 2: Do proactive tax planning

If you live in Canada, proactive tax planning should be one of your top priorities, because so much of our income could end up being allocated into taxes (30-50%) if we aren't paying attention to it and taking advantage of tax reduction strategies.

Your accountant is your best friend when it comes to tax planning. They are trained to know the various tax reduction strategies and can help you optimize the amount you are paying. One item to note is that not all account-ants proactively bring up tax reduction strategies with you – you may want to mention that you would like them to include tax planning as part of your accounting services engagement with them. Don't assume this is something that they would do for you as part of a tax filing service. The amount that you save from proactively tax planning is likely way more than what you would pay to the accountant and is worth your spending.

I recommend all business owners to have a general under-standing of how the Canadian marginal tax bracket works. You don't need to be a tax expert – but working with your accountant to understand how much tax is charged for each additional dollar that you earn is helpful. Find out how much you are paying in taxes personally and in your corporation, and look into strategies to reduce taxes payable.

Here are some questions to ask your accountant:

- How much tax am I paying each year in the corporation and personally?
- What average and marginal tax brackets am I in?
- What are some ways that I can optimize the tax that I pay now or in the future?
- For these suggested strategies, what are the pros and cons?
- What are your recommendations for my family and business' tax planning?

Doing proper tax planning may save hundreds to thousands to tens of thousands of dollars for your bottom line each year, and significantly change how much you can allocate towards savings and investments instead.

Principle 3: Avoid debt if you can

Should all debt be avoided? Or is there such a thing as good debt vs bad debt?

The main thing to know about debt is that it increases your financial risk, so you would want to weigh the probability of reward with the risk you are taking. What is the likelihood of earning a positive return from taking on the debt, knowing that you are 100% obligated to repay the debt?

Debt in your business

Depending on the type of business you have, debt may be necessary for purposes such as:

- Getting a short-term loan to pay for equipment and inventory in order to generate revenue growth. Debt is paid off with increased revenues.

- Getting a mortgage for a commercial property where your business is operating, instead of paying rent. In time, the mortgage will be paid off and commercial property will be worth multiple times what you paid for it.

- Getting a small business loan so you can hire more staff to keep up with the demand of your services or products, or to produce better products or more services. The loan is paid off with increased revenues.

- Paying your vendors and suppliers via corporate credit card, then fully paying off your credit card balances each month. You earn points and rewards without incurring high interest charges.

The above examples could be considered "good" debt, because the benefits of the loan outweigh the cost of borrowing.

There are also situations where you could borrow money, where the cost of borrowing outweighs the benefits. These are situations where you would likely be better off not to get into debt in the first place. Here are some examples:

- Needing to use your credit card or line of credit because you aren't making enough revenues each month to cover your operating costs such as payroll, taxes, and regular operating expenses. This may work for one month or two here and there, but if this happens regularly, it may indicate the business margins are too low to sustain a healthy operation.

- Getting a loan that doesn't result in generating a positive return over a reasonable period.

These may seem obvious, but I can assure you that many entrepreneurs are overly optimistic about how fast they will generate revenues from the expenses they have incurred. I've seen business owners get into trouble because they overestimated the amount of inventory they can sell, hired too many staff in too short a period, spent way more than necessary in building yet another website, or taking on long-term lease or debt obligations without considering potential fluctuations in revenues.

Personal debt

The principles for whether to take on debt in your business also apply in your personal life. Here are some situations where it may make sense to take on debt:

- Getting a mortgage to buy a home (as long as you can afford the mortgage repayments)

- Getting a lower interest rate loan to consolidate higher interest loans (e.g. credit card balances)

- Getting a loan to start, buy, or fund your business, as long as there are reasonable expectations that you will generate a positive return from the venture

- Financing education or certifications that results in increased income

Here are some situations where it may be questionable whether to take on debt:

- Using credit card or loan to pay for a lifestyle expense that can't be paid off with cash or savings (splurging on vacations, shopping, entertainment)

- Taking on debt to pay for a larger car, boat, or items that depreciate immediately after leaving the seller's lot

- Borrowing to invest in the stock market

I get asked quite a bit about the last item above – i.e. whether one should borrow money to invest. For example, if the interest rate is low at 3% and the stock market seems to be generating on average 10%, doesn't it make sense to borrow to invest? It helps to remember that interest rates and market returns fluctuate frequently. There is no guarantee that your investments will return what it did last year or the year before, and there is definitely a guarantee that you have to pay back the money that you borrowed.

Another item to consider with debt is that for every dollar that you borrow, you need to actually generate much more than a dollar to pay off that dollar. This is because personal debt is paid off with after-tax dollars.

Here is an example:

> If you borrow $1000 and the interest rate is 6%, you may think that you need to make $1,060 in order to pay off the loan ($1,000 borrowed amount plus $60 interest) after one year.

> In reality, if your average income tax rate is 30%, you need to generate $1,514 of personal income in order to pay off the original debt. This is because to generate $1,060 after tax, you need to generate $1,514 of income and then pay $454 of income tax.

Hence, it is actually costing you $60 of interest plus $454 of income taxes to pay back the $1,000 borrowed, which is more than 50% of what you borrowed!

Amount borrowed	$1,000	Income	$1,514
plus interest (6%)	$60	less Income taxes (30%)	$454
Amount to pay back after 1 year	**$1,060**	**After tax income required to pay off debt**	**$1,060**

If you aren't able to pay back the amount borrowed relatively quickly, the situation gets worse because now you owe more and more interest each year.

My advice to most clients is – really understand the cost and obligations of debt before using it as a vehicle in your financial planning. Use debt to fund emergencies or growth plans if you must and you have done your due diligence so that you can pay it back, but know that it is very easy to get into debt and often quite hard to get out of it if circumstances change in your business or in your personal life.

Principle 4: Save to meet short- and long-term goals

When your business becomes profitable, you are now at the stage where you have the ability to allocate funds towards the future rather than just focusing on paying the bills. When we think of the future, we may be considering short term, mid-term, or long term goals. The future could also bring unexpected circumstances that require financial margin so that we can sail through difficult seasons.

Here are some examples of goals to consider for your business:

Short-term goals:

- Save enough operating capital to cover regular expenses each month or each sales cycle

- Build an emergency fund to cover unexpected expenses or to cover expenses if revenues are down unexpectedly

Mid-term goals:

- Funding major purchases such as equipment upgrades, new products
- Funding education and training of key employees
- Funding expansion into new markets or new locations

Long term goals:

- To pay off commercial mortgages
- To start new companies or ventures

Similarly, in your personal financial planning, there may be short and long term goals:

- Having an emergency fund
- Pay off high-interest debt
- Save for children's education
- Save for major purchases (car, new home)
- Save for retirement
- Save for legacy wishes, to bestow gifts to charities or loved ones

Consider what goals you may want to work towards, how much is needed and by when, and start to allocate funds for these goals. My suggestion here is to consistently put money away for these goals and set up different accounts than the ones you use for daily banking or operations in your business. I find that business owners that keep their savings and operating accounts separate tend to be more likely to reach their goals. When the money is in a separate account, it is not as readily accessible so it doesn't get spent by accident, and it is also much easier to track progress and be encouraged by the consistent growth in savings.

Principle 5: Be generous with your giving

You may be wondering – Principles 1-4 make sense, since they all will allow you to keep more of what you make. How does being generous with your giving contribute to making good money decisions? And doesn't giving decrease the size of your pie?

I have found that this is one area in financial planning where we need to look beyond the stereotypical goal of saving as much as you can, or that he/she with the most amount accumulated wins.

Giving is the only mechanism that breaks the power of the love of money and frees you to use money as a means to achieve goals, rather than the goal itself. Within my clientele, those that are generous and give more to the charities and causes that they love are also more content and happier in life. They have a higher purpose in their work and in their life, because they are contributing and impacting others. They are more fulfilled personally, while their business reaps the social and financial benefits of giving – either with improved reputation, a more loyal and appreciative customer base and community, higher morale and engagement within their team, and yes, even tax benefits of giving. Some of my clients encourage their children from a young age to participate in giving as a family, and proactively select charities to volunteer or serve and give as a family. Philanthropy can be a great vehicle to bring family members closer together, to build character of generosity and citizenship, and to inspire the next generation to make an impact in the world.

There are many ways to give personally or through your business, including but not limited to the following:

- Giving cash to charities and causes

- Giving in kind (donating your products or services)

- Volunteering your time (or employee's time)

- Gifting of assets (publicly traded securities, real estate)

- Naming charities as beneficiaries in wills or insurance policies

- Setting up donor-advised funds

- Setting up a private foundation

Some of the strategies above allow donors to claim tax credits, which may result in substantial tax savings. The details of how to utilize these strategies are beyond the scope of this book, and I would suggest speaking with your financial advisor and accountant to learn more about how to set these up properly for your circumstances. Often, with proper counsel and planning, the timing and process of giving can be optimized to utilize the maximum available tax credits for charitable contributions.

Chapter 5:
Your Job Description
as a Business Owner

**Action: Understand the Business Owner
Job Description - to establish financial goals,
create appropriate business structures
and accountability measures to track
and guide your decision making.**

As your business grows, it is inevitable that your role will change along with the growth. In the earlier stages of your business, you may have spent most of your time doing marketing and sales and being a "technician", i.e. the delivery of your services or products. Over time, you may have hired employees or contractors and you shift to being more of a "manager". You no longer do all the work, but you are managing the work. As your business grows, you may even be needing to hire more managers, and now you are a "leader" managing managers.

There is typically a lot of training and resources available to help a business owner improve their skills on management and leadership. You may even have invested in training, courses, or business coaching that help improve your skills in leading and managing your team (if you haven't yet – this is an area that you may want to consider, as the skills for "doing" are very different from the skills needed for "managing" and "leading").

An additional topic that isn't as widely discussed, and fewer resources available, is the additional role and responsibilities as an Owner.

Ownership is not the same as Leadership.

You may be wondering – if I own my company, isn't it the same as leading my company? What is the difference? Why does it matter?

The reason why I dedicated this whole chapter to Ownership is that this area is so often overlooked. In addition to leading the team, here are additional roles and responsibilities of an "Owner" that should be included in your job description:

- Establish ownership vision and goals
- Create accountability structures
- Identify company benchmark and goals
- Establish ownership policies

Role 1: Establish Ownership Vision and Goals

The owner in the business is responsible for determining the vision and goals of the company. In the early stages, a company's main goal may be to reach a certain amount of revenue so that there are sufficient funds to pay expenses and compensate the owner appropriately. Once this goal is reached, vision and goal setting become more of an art, rather than science. Owners have choices about who they want to be, where they want to take the company, and how they want to get there.

Your role as an owner is to contemplate vision and goal questions such as these:

- Who do we want to be?
- Where do we want to be 1 year, 3 year, 5 years from now or beyond?
- How do we measure success?
- How fast do we want to grow? How much risk are we willing to take on?

There are no right or wrong answers to these questions. The answers may come to you immediately, or it may take some soul searching and reflection. The answers to these questions are important because they frame what financial planning strategies are appropriate for the owner and for the business.

For example, I had two clients who were both incredibly talented interior designers, however they couldn't have had more drastically different visions for their business. One of them, Sarah, knew that she wanted to grow her company as fast as possible to include residential and commercial (restaurants and retail) design services, and grow her team of interior designers to have the ability to take on more than 20 projects at the same time. Another client, Anna, wanted to focus on delivering on just 1-2 residential projects at a time, so that she could attend to the details herself and not "stress" too much.

The financial planning strategies for these two companies are different. Sarah's focus is on growth in her company, so decisions were made to allocate most of the company's profit back into marketing efforts and hiring and growing her team. She paid herself only a modest salary for a number of years, took on more risk via business loans to fund company growth, and eventually reaped the benefits of her vision when she was acquired by a mid-size construction management company that wanted to expand their interior design offerings.

Anna's financial planning looked different from Sarah's. First of all, she paid herself more since she had fewer overhead and expenses. She also needed to allocate more funds to her short-term savings since there were occasions where she was in-between projects and didn't have any income. We also allocated more funds for retirement savings as it is unlikely that her firm, being structured as a sole owner operator, will be acquired by an external party in the future.

Role 2. Create Accountability Structures

Accountability is where "the rubber meets the road". Most business owners have amazing vision and know intrinsically how to start something, but some struggle with accountability and finishing things well, especially when it comes to areas in the business that seem tedious and not very exciting.

It is easy to think that "I'm the boss in my business, I can do whatever I want! That's why I quit working for someone else in the first place." While that may be true, what I know is that we are all human, and all humans have blind spots. Do you know what your blind spots are? Would it be helpful to think about what measures you want to put in place for your own good?

I once worked with a business owner (who is, sadly, no longer in business today) who quit his job as a salesperson for a security staffing company to start his own firm. He had been the top sales person for years with his previous employer, and became frustrated over time about how things were run. He had a vision for what he wanted to provide for his clients, but his company always responded with "we don't have the resources for that". When we met, he was in early years in his business – very optimistic and very excited about what was to come.

He had engaged me shortly after starting his business to review his financials and projections and to provide commentary on whether he was on track, and whether any adjustments were needed.

When I reviewed his financials and projections, I couldn't help but think that his revenue projections seemed very optimistic, and the associated pace of buying equipment and hiring security guards seemed risky if things didn't work out. Another item which alarmed me was that his staff needed to be paid 30-60 days ahead of when his accounts with clients would be settled. In sharing these concerns with him, he dismissed most of the caution, mentioning those were industry norms and that he wasn't too concerned because he was really confident in his ability to sell.

Well, he is no longer in business today, and when I checked his profile on LinkedIn recently, he is now back to being a salesperson working for a different company in the same industry, which is unfortunate as he truly wanted to be a business owner instead of an employee.

As a business owner, it is helpful to know what your strengths and weaknesses are. Are you strong in sales but weak in financials? Are you great at expanding to new markets, but get bored with serving your existing markets after a while? Are you amazing at delivering excellent customer service, but struggle with invoicing clients in a timely manner?

Most business owners I know need to put some support in place to create accountability structures to guard against their weaker areas. Here are some areas of financial accountability areas to consider for the company:

- Accounts Payable and Receivables – ensuring that bills are paid and invoices and payments are received on time

- Cash Flow – ensuring that cash inflow can meet timing for cash outflow

- Profitability – ensuring that expenses are less than revenues

- Compensation policies – determining how much to pay owners/employees, when dividends would be paid to shareholders

- Risk management – mitigating losses in case of sickness/death of key people in the company, insurance to cover loans and debt, unforeseen circumstances like fire, theft, injuries, professional liability or other industry and business specific risks

Another area of importance is setting up your company's operational structure and policies that define the relationship with business partners. These may include the following items:

- Determining shares structures (voting vs. non-voting partners)

- Establishing shareholder agreements including buy-sell provisions (i.e. who can become partners in the future, what happens if a partner wants to exit etc.)

- Setting up employment contracts for employees and working owners on role descriptions and expectations

- Setting up client and supplier contracts, if applicable

If some of these items seem overwhelming or foreign, that is normal. Most of these items (and more that are not mentioned here) are usually done with the counsel of your accountant and lawyer. While it is tempting to leave it to them to figure out the details, the truth is that ownership of getting these items done is part of the owner's job description.

Role 3. Identify Company Benchmarks and Goals

Peter Drucker, the father of management thinking, has a great quote: "What gets measured gets managed." I've found this to be so true for business owners. If you want to see something happen in your company, you need to track and measure it.

Your role as owner in the company includes setting goals and determining what metrics ought to be used to measure progress towards these goals. The most basic goals may include the following:

Goals	Description	Purpose
Revenue	Amount of sales over a period of time (monthly, quarterly, yearly etc.)	Tracks the sales coming into the company, and whether sales trends over time are healthy.
Profit	Revenue minus expenses. Being profitable enables you to have surplus	Tracks whether your company is spending less than what it is making, gives you insights to

Goals	Description	Purpose
	funds to allocate towards paying bonuses/dividends, use funds for expansion, or increase amount of reserves to weather uncertain times in future	make decisions about how to optimize pricing, what product/services to add or drop, and what expenses to increase or reduce in order to better run your company.
Profit Margin	Profit as a percentage of total revenues.	This allows you to gauge financial health in your business over multiple years. As your revenues grow, are your profits growing proportionally because your expenses are well managed? Or are your expenses increasing at a faster rate than your revenues?
Cash Flow	Amount of cash needed over a period of time to pay expenses	Income and cash coming into the company may not always align with when expenses need to be paid. Being aware of how much cash comes in and how much cash goes out and the associated timing allows you to avoid not being able to pay your bills.

While the above are likely standard financial goals that every company would have, there are many additional financial goals, metrics, and financial ratios that may be helpful for your specific industry or stage of business.

Here are some financial ratios and what they are used for. The specifics of each are beyond the scope of this book, but I wanted to include them so that you are encouraged to think about what types of metrics may be useful for your company, and to start tracking them.

Category	Purpose	Examples
Profitability Ratios	Measures how well a company manages its expenses in order to generate a profit, given the level of revenue.	Gross Profit Margin Operating Margin Net Profit Margin Return on Equity Return on Assets
Liquidity Ratios	Measures the amount of liquidity (i.e. cash) available in the company to cover payment obligations.	Current Ratio Quick Ratio Cash Ratio
Efficiency Ratios	Measures how efficient the company is using its assets to generate sales.	Inventory Turnover Ratio Receivables Turnover Ratio Average Collection Period Sales per Employee
Solvency Ratios	Measures how well a company can meet its debt obligations.	Debt Ratio Debt to Equity Ratio Times Interest Earned Ratio Debt Service Coverage Ratio

Think of financial metrics like a car's dashboard. When you are driving, your car's dashboard tells you whether you are going too fast, or if you are almost out of fuel, and if it is overheating on a hot summer's day. There are even indicators in some cars that will tell you that your car tire's pressure is low, or that you are now 2 weeks past the time to bring the car in for service. Ultimately, metrics are there to help give an indication of where you are, whether you are on the right track, and warn you if you are heading into danger.

Your homework is to determine, perhaps together with your accountant or Chief Financial Officer (CFO), what goals you want to set in the company, and what you will track and measure to let you know whether you are on track or off track on these goals.

4. Establish Ownership Policies

We are all likely more familiar with having policies that govern employees in the company rather than policies that govern owners. After all, you are the boss in the company, and you can do whatever you want with your company, right?

That is absolutely right. You can, of course, not structure any policies for the owners of the company so that you have complete flexibility to change anything in the company as you see fit. However, what I know is that not all owners are created nor trained with sufficient discipline to act in the best interest of the long-term success and viability of the company. We are all humans, and prone to occasionally make emotional, on-a-whim, short-term-focused decisions that may not benefit our longer-term goals.

Here are some real examples of decisions that business owners I know have made, and then come to regret down the road:

- Hired a close friend for a position in their company instead of posting a job opening

- Decided to launch a new division and a new product line without doing marketing research

- Paid themselves a bonus without checking the company cash flow, because they needed the funds for an upcoming family trip

- Decided to not file income tax yet because they haven't caught up on book-keeping

- Bought $80,000 of additional inventory because the supplier put them on a "super sale", without looking deeper into their existing inventory levels or turnover times

The outcome is that these decisions usually caused additional turmoil in the company that often turned into cash flow problems, and the owner then had to focus their attention to fix the fire, instead of having their attention on growing the company.

While a company that is owned by a single owner may not need a long list of policies since the owner can make decisions independently without consult, any companies that have multiple partners would benefit from having a more structured approach with ownership decisions such as:

- When and how dividends are declared and paid

- Role and responsibility of owners and the associated compensation structure

- Approval process for committing to capital expenditures or large purchases

- When to take on debt

- Hiring of family, relatives, or friends into the company

- Who can be future owners in the company, how will shares be purchased or passed on by existing owners

- How to exit as an owner, either voluntarily (e.g. retirement) or involuntarily (disagreement, illness, premature death)

- How to come to a decision if owners don't agree with each other

- How to set and uphold common vision, values, and goals for the company

For businesses with multiple owners, it is inevitable that you will have differences in opinion. Every partnership starts off in the honeymoon phase, but ultimately as the partners' vision and preferences evolve over time, having internal policies that spell out how potential issues should be identified, discussed, and handled could help avoid unnecessary conflicts within the company. Many of the above ownership policies can and should be spelled out in a shareholder agreement, with the counsel of your business lawyer.

Chapter 6: Align Financial Planning with Your Vision for Growth

Action: Discern what type of business you want to build and align your financial strategies to your growth plans.

Your financial planning strategies should be derived from, and support and fund, the strategic growth goals you set for yourself, your family, and your business.

The level of complexity of financial planning is highly dependent on the type of business you are trying to build and the stage of business that you are in.

"What is your vision of the company? What do you want your company to do financially?"

I find that in the financial planning industry, these questions are often neglected. Unless you are working with financial advisors that have a comprehensive or holistic approach and not just focusing on pitching products, it is easy to end up having financial strategies that are off-the-shelf and cookie-cutter.

Your advisor's financial planning process should include a comprehensive needs discovery, including asking you questions about your business and where you are planning to take the business, and how you plan to get there. Your personal and business financial planning strategies should be directly designed based on your specific phase of business and where you want to take the business.

In the table below, you will find three different types of business, and some typical associated goals and values of the business owner:

Business Type	Description	Goals and Values
Lifestyle	The business that is centered around the owner, geared towards supporting the owner's income needs and work preferences rather than increasing revenues	Simplicity Low overhead Freedom and flexible schedule Work to live rather than live to work

Business Type	Description	Goals and Values
Organic Growth	The business is focused on increasing stakeholder value, growth via expansion of markets or products/services	Grow with purpose to increase value for customers, employees, and/or their community Growth for the sake of delivering better solution to more customers/clients
Fast Scale	The business is focused on increasing volume exponentially. Growth via mergers and acquisitions and leveraging external equity or debt	Market domination Fast growth and shareholder value maximization Grow with eventual goal of exit and liquidity

Which business type resonates more with you? In my experience, if asked, business owners typically gravitate towards one of the above in their current business. Some may have started with creating one type and then find that their vision evolved over time to another type.

The focus and strategies of your financial planning would vary, depending on your business type and the associated pace of growth. The following section outlines some of the goals and strategies that may be applicable for each different type of business.

Financial planning for lifestyle businesses

A business owner with a lifestyle business likely wants a business that avoids the burdens of managing a large number of people, allows them to balance the demands of their work with their non-business goals and pursuits, and allows them to do work that they love, building products or delivering services directly to their clients.

Since the owner is primarily involved in the delivery of the goods/services, it is rare that a lifestyle business can be sold. Revenues are directly correlated with how many hours the owner is putting into the business, so the most profitable path is to have the owner keep getting better at what they do and making more income per hour for as long as they can.

Financial strategies for lifestyle businesses may include:

- Increase dollars made per hour by either increasing expertise to charge more, or become more efficient at what they do

- Control expenses to allow income to sufficiently pay expenses and salary to owner

- Save money to cover for periods where owner isn't working

- Consistently save and invest for retirement since business is unlikely to be sold, to prepare for time when owner either cannot work or chooses not to work

Financial planning for organic growth businesses

Business owners focusing on Organic Growth want to not only make an income for themselves, but also, they feel a calling or a drive to deliver better solutions to more and more clients. They want to grow, not just for the sake of growing, but that they feel the need to provide more value to their customers over time. They are continuously getting better and more unique at how they deliver products and services, with the goal to be "best" at what they do and, and at the same time, balance the interests of their stakeholders, which include their customers but may expand to include employees, owners, vendors, and their communities.

A key distinction of this type of business is that they are typically privately held, in order to allow the owners to maintain their own control and freedom, and to protect the ability to uphold their values and not be subjected to growth or shareholder value maximization pressures, especially if such pursuits compromise the quality and essence of what they do.

When it comes to financial planning for these businesses, here are some strategies that may be appropriate:

- Determine how best to allocate profit, i.e. what amount should be allotted to owners' compensation vs. reinvesting back to the business

- Intentionally allocate funds to increase customer value, invest into employees, or into initiatives that give back to the community to align with company values and mission

- Owner succession planning, recognizing that with a unique, purpose-driven business, it may be challenging to find external buyers who honor the original vision. It is likely that employees and internally developed talent who have been living the culture of the firm can more easily carry on the business in the future (for example, employee stock ownership plans may work better here for succession)

- As business grows to include more owners and partners that (hopefully) share in the firm's vision, to look into governance structures and decision making processes that promotes effective communication and reduces conflicts

Financial planning for fast scale businesses

Fast Scale businesses are exactly as it sounds – the business is focused on growing and expanding the company as fast as possible. Growth can come organically from marketing efforts, via expanding products and services offered, or expanding to different regions, countries, or continents. Growth can also come inorganically, from mergers or acquisitions of competitors or other companies providing complementary products and services.

Financial planning for these companies needs to consider that circumstances change very quickly over short periods of time. The company may be bringing on clients rapidly and hiring rapidly, so internal systems and operations need to change to accommodate the speed of growth. In order to sustain this pace, external funding (either debt or equity) may be used to achieve company goals. Often, the eventual goal for the owners of the company is a liquidity event – to either sell to a larger firm, a strategic buyer, a private equity firm, or to go public with an Initial Public Offering (IPO).

Here are some financial planning considerations:

- Know how fast the company is "burning money" i.e. the amount needed to sustain operation expenses each month and how best to reduce the burn rate, extend cash runway, or manage expenses

- Founders and owners to prepare funds for their own personal needs as they are likely not going to be paying themselves very much while building the company

- Understanding the pros and cons for debt vs equity financing

- Having a 2-3 year financial plan that outlines company goals, revenue projections, headcount needs, major expenses, and working capital required

- Focusing on having financial dashboards and Key Performance Indicators (KPI's) to track results and whether executing well against plans

- Upon liquidity or sale of the company, to determine best use of sale proceeds for owners' financial and retirement planning and funding of future ventures

In essence, once your company is profitable, it is important to determine your vision and the type of company that you want to build, instead of accidentally finding that you have a company that forces you to take on new roles due to the growth demands, and that these roles are not necessarily what you want to do (e.g. managing employees, taking on debt or additional partners or external equity to grow).

While the types of companies listed in this chapter is by no means exhaustive, I'm hoping that outlining these three examples give you a hint of what you want to build. There is probably one type that resonates more with you than the others. There is no right or wrong type of growth, and it may be that in different seasons of your life, different types of company growth structures would appeal to you.

Once you have chosen the type of company you are building, you can now consider how your finances can be organized accordingly. I would recommend sharing your vision and your goals with your financial advisors, so that they can customize strategies in the different financial planning areas (tax planning, cash flow planning, investment, insurance, retirement, estate planning etc.) to support your current and future needs.

Chapter 7:
Putting It Together

From the previous chapters, you've gleaned some insights into the specific areas of financial planning to consider. Where do you go from here?

Perhaps we can support you in your next chapter. What I've realized is that for most business owners, they would rather focus on the business development, marketing, sales, or operations of their business. Financial planning is akin to a necessary evil – it's really not that exciting for most business owners, but the appropriate systems and strategies need to be implemented and managed in order for you to achieve your business goals.

I'm usually not a client's first financial planner. When clients contact our team, they usually already have some of the financial pieces in place, but they don't feel confident that they have the full picture of how it all works together. They're not sure that they're being strategic in their finances. What we do is take a look at each of the financial planning areas, determine what is working well and what is no longer effective, collaborate with clients to determine priorities and then roll up our sleeves and tackle each area that needs adjustments.

For example, here are some of the items we take a look at:

- Review financial statements and discuss how best to adjust your revenues and expenses to improve profitability

- Determine business and personal cash flow requirements

- Work with your tax accountant (or introduce you to one in our network, if needed) to optimize tax planning

- Work with your lawyer (or refer you to one) to ensure that your corporate and personal legal documents are in good order. This may include restructuring of your company, setting up a holding company, finally getting employment contracts, partnership shareholder agreements, or wills and powers of attorney in place.

- Determine with you how best to allocate profit in your business, depending on your personal goals and business growth trajectory

- Review your insurance planning to reduce financial risks and ensure your business and your family are taken care of in case of unexpected circumstances

- Create and monitor your retirement planning base on potential exit strategies for your business in the future

- Grow your wealth by helping you invest in diversified assets (investment portfolio, real estate, business ventures, insurance assets)

- Meet with you regularly to offer input and counsel on changes in your business, industry, or support you and help to navigate financial changes that come from seasons of change in your life, whether anticipated or unexpected, whether positive or negative

We do this via structured planning meetings and coaching calls, and strive to balance between a structured approach to get you to your goals, while maintaining enough flexibility to allow changes in goals or vision over time. Our company is built with a team that believes highly in strong implementation and execution, so we don't build financial plans that become obsolete the moment you leave our meeting. Instead, we prefer to refer to ourselves as your financial co-pilots. You are ultimately in charge of your destination, but we will be along for the journey, to point out the dangers along the way, or provide you with objective information so that you can be confident and have clarity in your financial planning.

If there is a small part of you that feels that you could find more clarity and confidence with our help than what you are currently doing, perhaps we should chat. If you are like me, and the thought of moving forward from what you are doing probably feels somewhat daunting, I have two suggestions:

1. Take the Financially Smart Business Assessment

The Financially Smart Business Assessment will show you what's currently missing in your business or personal finances, and help you quickly see what opportunities there are for improvement and how best to prioritize these areas. The assessment takes an average of five minutes to complete, and we'll send you your results once you're done.

To take the Financially Smart Business Assessment, please go to: www.financiallysmartbusiness.com

2. Request a collaborative discovery session so we can chat about your financial planning

There is no obligation to work with us. In this session, we go over your goals, priorities, and concerns, and we will share our process and philosophy of financial planning in more detail, in order to see if it would make sense to work together.

Book your discovery session at www.financiallysmartbusiness.com.

If you are at the stage of business where you feel that you don't have a good picture of whether you are doing ok financially or if you are on the right track, you will find this discovery session very helpful.

Over the years, I've found that just that one discovery session can make the difference and change your financial life for the better. We offer a safe, confidential, non-judgemental space to discuss your finances that you may have hesitated to share with others. We're here with a warm approach, and we offer a compassionate ear to listen to your particular struggles and help you figure out what are the best next steps.

Go to www.financiallysmartbusinesss.com and schedule your Collaborative Discovery session after answering a few simple questions. These will help us to be on our way to solving your problems, and give you more details about our approach.

About the Author

Felicia is usually not someone's first financial planner. People come see her when they need to graduate to the next level of financial planning.

Before becoming a financial planner, Felicia spent 6 years as a business coach to over 200 business owners who grossed between $200K – $5M. This gave her a front row seat to noticing how making money doesn't always translate to keeping the money.

She watched many smart people generate good revenue, while on the flip side, not being strategic about what to do with the money they were making, to live the flexible future that they most wanted.

She became a financial planner because she noticed that as her client's finances grew and they were working harder, they weren't sure they were gaining ground financially to meet the future that they envisioned for themselves.

Her approach to financial planning may look different from a typical financial planner. For starters, her insight as a business coach and the tested ability to navigate the complexities of growing a business or practice is married with financial planning competencies.

With her engineering background, her left brain is trained to analyze, evaluate, and create solutions, while her right brain is seasoned from years of coaching to help clients clarify and navigate to the big picture.

About Clarity Planning Inc.

Clarity Planning Inc. is a financial planning firm that provides financial insights and direction for business owners, incorporated professionals, and their families.

Our Values

- We meet you where you are at without judgement, and come along as a guide.
- We bring clarity through proactive education and communication
- We do our work with care and excellence
- We take a holistic approach and work collaboratively with your advisors
- We embrace growth and learning to increase our capacity to serve

Our Service Offerings

- Financial Planning
- Investment Management
- Business Financial Coaching
- Insurance Planning
- Retirement Planning
- Succession and Exit Planning
- Family Enterprise Planning
- Estate Planning

Manufactured by Amazon.ca
Bolton, ON